The Secrets of Crowdfunding

A Step-by-Step Guide to Getting the Most
from Your Kickstarter Campaign

Sean Akers

ISBN: 978-0988322318

Published by Sean Akers.
Also Available in e-Book format.

www.secretsofcrowdfunding.com
www.seanakers.com

.

Crowdfunding is the process of gathering financial support for a project. Pretty simple. The concept isn't new. People buy and sell stock in companies every day. But with crowdfunding websites, the concept has reached a much more personal audience.

Let's be clear, getting involved in a project is not buying a piece of ownership or reaping the benefits of the financial success of that project. That kind of business transaction is highly regulated. In the US, it is the Securities and Exchange Commission who monitor and manage the business of shared ownership. Using Indiegogo or Kickstarter to sell "stock" in your company or project is currently prohibited. Though the laws are changing, the system is not in place to sell ownership.

However, offering "rewards" for financial contribution is merely sale of product. If someone wants to support your project in exchange for a t-shirt, they may choose to do that. That is simple commerce. In fact, crowdfunding through these sites is really just ordering a product before it is created. It take a bit of patience and a bit of faith. And it takes money.

And that is the whole reason that site after site is being launched to help facilitate the crowdfunding process. What does the site owner get? A percentage of money raised. What do the project creators get? A venue to share their project and raise finances without the technical hangups of trying to build their own e-commerce website.

When it comes to the thousands of projects online, waiting to be discovered and successfully funded, the most important factor is the project itself. You may have a project that you really believe in, but it up to the crowd to decide whether or not the project has merit.

THIS BOOK WILL NOT...

• judge whether or not your project will appeal to the masses.

THIS BOOK WILL...

• prepare you for a crowdfunding campaign

• help you to calculate your real financial goals and budget

• guide you in setting your levels of support and the rewards at each level

• advise you on planning a communication strategy for the campaign

• demonstrate how to organize information to best serve the project

• enable you to entice visitors to become supporters

Sean Akers is a teacher, a techie, and a film producer. He designs websites for artists, authors, and musicians. He studies new technologies to help better promote and market his clients. He works with Before The Door Pictures to make films that tell great stories.

As crowdfunding sites have grown in popularity, Sean has been tracking the failures and successes on many sites. He is a supporter of over 60 projects on Kickstarter.com and several projects on other sites.

As a consultant, he has helped make several projects reach and exceed their goals. His work with Sian Heder on DOG EAT DOG raised over $30,000 on a $7,500 goal. With Jake Walden, SAME SOMETHING DIFFERENT raised over $20,000 on a $10,000 goal. Matthew Allard and Chris New's TICKING raised over $13,000 on a $5000 goal.

Other project creators have consulted Sean for advice on how to make sure they budget correctly and how they should build their page so that people commit to support.

This book is the culmination of years of research. When these principles are practically applied, there hasn't been a project yet that hasn't at least reached its goal. The average for Sean's projects is raising over 200% of the Kickstarter goal.

For the sake of this book, I am going to refer specifically to Kickstarter rather than just crowdfunding. It is the most popular site for a wide range of projects, restricts projects to a set of guidelines and requires that projects meet a financial goal to be funded.

Other sites may offer different services or fewer restrictions. But for the sake of this guide, I will refer to the crowdfunding site as Kickstarter.

Preparing For The Campaign

When you decide to bring your project to the public in a Kickstarter campaign, you are committing to a larger scale of work than just producing a short film or manufacturing a gadget. You are putting your work into three different phases.

Project 1: Fundraising

The first is the fundraising phase. In this phase you research and develop your concepts so that you have enough information to know a real budget and timeline for production of the second phase. In this phase, you also plan and launch your Kickstarter campaign.

Project 2: Production

Once you have met the necessary goals and raised the funds, you move to the second phase. In this phase you bring your creation to life. That means, that you use part of the funds to create or build or paint or print your product. (Don't get turned off by the word "product." It is just a fact that you are making something that will be delivered to your supporters. It doesn't take away the art of what you are doing.)

Project 3: Delivery

When you reach the point where your garage is filled with DVDs or the printer has just finished stapling and folding your first comic book, then you move on to fulfillment. This phase is labor intensive, especially if you have a lot of supporters and you don't plan on paying for help. It is incredibly important that you are able to deliver on your promise. Crowdfunding relies on your supporters' trust and your trustworthiness.

Once you have decided what your project is going to be, you need to identify several factors in the development of your Kickstarter campaign.

What makes your project different?

The first consideration is making sure that you project isn't a duplicate of another project. If your film is about a space farmer who decides to enlist in the resistance army against a galactic empire, then you are probably getting into a danger zone. It is very important in the long run that you are bringing a new take or idea to life.

Marketing guru Seth Godin calls this "The Purple Cow." If you are sitting on a train, riding along in the countryside and looking out the window, then you will probably see farmland with cows grazing. One cow doesn't look too different from another. But if you were to see a purple cow, then you would notice immediately. That is the goal of marketing... to make your product the standout.

In a Kickstarter campaign, it is the standout project that gets the attention. And it gets the money.

Find the elements of your project that make it unique. Those elements are the key to getting people to notice and support you.

Find your key audience

Once you know what makes you different, you can take the steps to find out who your best potential customers would be. If you make an iPhone case, then your primary audience will be iPhone owners. In that group, you are looking for people who either don't have a case or believe that your case is better than the one that they currently use. So the market of all mobile phone users is limited to iPhone users. Then it is limited again to people who want to use a case. So the audience gets smaller and smaller.

Is that bad, to narrow the audience? In a way, it gives you a better idea of the number of potential customers you might reach. And of course, in your campaign, you won't be reaching all of those people. You may not even reach 10% of them. But if you reach enough of them and differentiate yourself, then you will certainly have a better chance of finding people willing to support your campaign.

Identify channels of communication

Knowing your potential customers will guide you to specific sources of news and entertainment that would be of interest to them. This is targeted marketing. You seek your target and plan your marketing campaign to reach them through the blogs and social sites that they already frequent. If your project is broad, then you might have a harder time marketing. A well-made t-shirt is a very broad concept, since nearly everyone buys t-shirts. But a t-shirt with a print of Shakespeare on it would be more narrowly marketed, since literature buffs and English majors are more likely to buy the shirt than football fans or elementary school children.

Look for blogs that would normally appeal to your audience as a way to get the campaign to them. The blog might cover the campaign, since it is appealing to them. Blogs may also allow you to advertise on their site, which is an expense, but a targeted method of reaching people.

Source your materials, service providers, or team

When you make a series of art prints, you need to find out where to buy ink and paper. And you need the specific costs. If your project is recording an album, you need to find a studio and musicians. If you are making a wristband for your iPod so you can wear it like a watch, then you need to find a facility to mold and cast the band.

In a short film, you will need to find locations and crew members, purchase permits and file paperwork. If you are developing a videogame, you will need computers, artists and programmers to bring the game from concept to beta and then release.

Sourcing your materials, crew, or your service providers will help you to identify your real costs. Put all of the costs into a budget, which you will use later in planning your campaign.

Space

Make sure that you are considering work space in your budget. Whether that is a temporary office or workshop, you should plan so that you are capable of doing the work. Some projects might not need more than a corner of your bedroom for some paperwork. If you need 5 employees, you need to provide them a space to work comfortably and professionally. A home office is fine. A garage birthed the Apple brand. There are plenty of options. But make sure that you cover yourself.

Create a timeline

Knowing the project as you do, plan a timeline for each phase of the work. Create benchmarks along the way, so that you know that you are reaching goals. Give yourself more time than the bare minimum, but be reasonable about getting the project completed. You want to bring your idea to life and share it with your supporters quickly enough that they are willing to pay in advance.

3. Building Project Confidence

What you are developing in the planning phase of your work is a brand identity. The key is to be yourself. Be honest about what you are creating and what it is.

Proving your ability

If you are making a usb device, then you need to create a model or a working prototype,to demonstrate your work.

If you are a film-maker, your product is a film. You MUST create a video for the site that shows that you are capable of making a film.

A musician can create their brand identity by sharing 30 second demo tracks. Or they can share some of their previous work.

An artist can show samples, sketches, early planning.

Give it a name

Give your project a name. A device with a name or logo on it gives it a professional feel. It gives it an identity. And all the information you share about the gadget and its capabilities become part of the brand identity.

An untitled album or film seems really obscure. It can make an audience feel as if the creator doesn't really know where they are going. A list of tracks for the album, a synopsis of the film, or a set of storyboards can do wonders for the project.

Throughout the process of fundraising, production and delivery, you are going to need to keep your supporters connected. Updates through Kickstarter and emails to your supporters will make a huge difference in the campaign. You will keep the supporters engaged and interested. And you can let them know if there are problems without worry. If you update them at milestones, you can be honest about slow downs in production or problems in coding a level of the game, booking the recording studio, or scheduling actors.

The content will need to be specific to your project. But consider a photograph of the first day of shooting your short. Look for moments that will be of interest. The wristband being molded. The process of inking a page of the comic book.

Look to your team for more content. Each member of your team is a different face that you can share. If you need to go to China to visit a production facility, then take pictures and share them. If you are sculpting models in your garage, take pictures of the progress. Grab a couple shots of the band setting up in the studio for a day of recording.

Inclusion the process is one of the major reasons that people get involved early. A film lover in Kansas wants to have the Hollywood experience. An art lover in Georgia wants to see the clay become the creature. The geek in Pittsburgh wants to watch her iPhone case being molded. The fan in Vienna wants to hear a bit of your next single before anyone else.

Kickstarter, IndieGoGo and other sites show their successful and failed projects in the site. A quick search can reveal someone who made millions and someone else who missed the mark.

The data in that site shows how many supporters got involved, over what time period, and the levels of their support. You can see if people give $1 or $1000.

When looking for examples of success, you want to look at all of the elements.

The videos

Look at the videos to see how they are produced. Some are really creative and others are very straightforward. Some rely on a warm narrator, while others rely on a great sense of humor.

When you look at the videos of failed sites, you will likely a range from good to bad. The video doesn't make the project. But it can certainly break it.

The text

Really direct and well organized content in the main body is important. Longer text without breaks, text without images, or very little text are all bad news.

The rewards

People set their rewards at different levels. In some cases, you get a DVD for $10 in support. In other cases, it is the $100 level that gets you a DVD. Unless your film is made of solid gold, the DVD isn't worth $100. See what else they have offered to get supporters to pay that much. See where failed projects missed the mark on pricing their support levels and where their offerings are so vanilla that no one even bothers to get involved.

What do you have that an audience might want? What area of specific interest are you appealing to?

[handwritten: Get Catherine to do a film]

Known talents and interests

In one of my projects, Dog Eat Dog, we planned as short film that starred Zachary Quinto, the actor who plays Spock in the new Star Trek movies. That was a great benefit to the project. Zach has fans worldwide. And those fans got involved. But we learned something else. The short film was about dog rescue. And more people got involved in the Kickstarter because they, too, had rescued their pet. There was something more powerful than the star. There was an emotional connection to the content of the film.

Another successful project on Kickstarter was a magazine for Soccer fans. The project got a great deal of support from fans of the sport, but also got support from people who thought that the concept of the magazine was really cool.

Reasons to support

I have and continue to support many projects on Kickstarter. Some I support for the friends who are involved. Others I support because they feature a talent I like. But mostly, I support projects that I think are really cool.

Find your strengths. See if there is something that makes your project relatable to people beyond soccer fans or Spock lovers. Find the emotional connections with your potential audience. Use these things in the entire campaign. If you are lucky enough to create something that people think is cool, then they will jump on the chance to get involved.

[handwritten: 250 / $200 – Drawing of your pet]

Setting Your Financial Goals

When you create your budget, you are planning for several things. It isn't just production of the project, it is paying for your team, workspace and storage. It is making sure that you are prepared to ship all of the rewards to your supporters.

Leave room in your budget

When you create a budget, leave a little room for problems. Contingency budget is a little extra to make sure that you are covered for unforeseen expenses.

If your project is a film, then you want to have some extra money in case you need an extra day of shooting or post-production color correction. If you are making an album, your contingency might allow you some extra money to make sure your mix and mastering it the best that it can be.

Sure, you want to keep your budget low, but you want to protect your supporters by ensuring that you have enough money to complete the project and deliver on your promises.

Help from a pro

If you have an opportunity to look at budgets from other people, do it. Look at another short film budget. See if there is someone who has created a gadget and look at their planning budget. Have an expert, or someone who has more experience than you do, look over your budget to double-check your work.

If you don't have an expert or a comparison, because your project is so different, like a new game system or gadget, then make sure that your costs are entirely covered and that you have additional funds if the scope of the project changes or if one of your sources craps out.

Even the most successful projects run into problems. If your campaign in 10 times more successful than you thought, can your sources create what you need? Are there limits to what a provider can output for you? Do you have enough people to make sure that you can complete the job?

If you overachieve on the project, you should have significantly more profit margin, so you might be protected. But you need to make sure that it doesn't sink the project.

8. Choosing Service Providers

When you are considering your service providers and sourcing materials, make sure that you are planning for both your minimum and maximum capacities.

When TikTok and LunaTik wristbands, created to hold the iPod Nano as if it were a wristwatch, were launched on Kickstarter, the plan was to get enough people to love the idea that the creators could cover the tooling and setup costs and then produce enough to meet the demand of their supporters. It was planned as a $15,000 goal. The first success of its kind, the campaign hit $942,578. That was a huge difference in the number of products that needed to be created.

The one thing that many successful Kickstarters say, in retrospect, is that they wish that they would have planned better for success.

The best way to be prepared for success is to know the limitations of the supply chain and the service providers. If your supplier can only produce 1000 gadgets, then that is your limit on the campaign. A backup provider, who could do 5000 or more, would be good to have in your pocket.

In a film situation, making the film is really important. If you exceed your minimum, you can choose to put more money on screen, hire more crew or bigger talent, or even pay your crew better. But if you need to produce 1000 dvds to complete your obligations, then that cost needs to be offset by the contributors. And the service provider who was doing 50 burned DVDs might not be your best choice. A replicator doing a run of 1000 would be much more cost effective.

Make sure that you are including legal and accounting costs. There may be situations in which trademarking a name, creating contracts, or tackling cash flow become more than you can handle. Professional help may not be cheap, but it may become a necessity.

Look at all of your costs, from packaging the product to shipping materials. Know where you can go to get more, if it is possible. Don't let success hurt you.

9. Chart your costs

A great way to visualize how your project will work is to chart the costs of the project at different levels of support. For example, if you create an iPhone case, you will have a lot of base costs, like creating the model and the cast.

Once base / startup costs are covered, then individual items have their own cost. The materials, printing, packaging, and other elements will add up to a cost for each item.

If you make 100 of those cases, the cost will be much more per item than making 1000. So if you make a chart of the costs, you can see where you need to be at each level of production to break even. Once you do that, you can see where you need to begin setting your financial goals.

If the startup cost is in creating artwork, an album or a film, then the per-unit costs are in creating the prints, CDs, DVDs, and other reward items for each person.

Sample chart: Start-up Costs

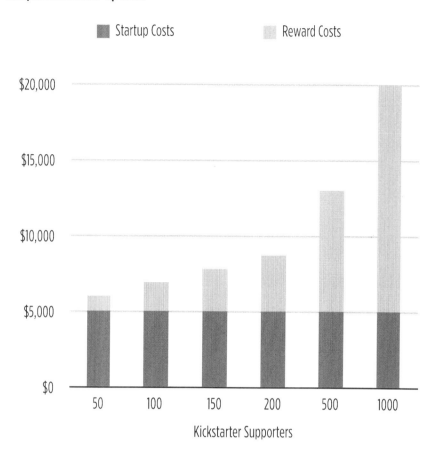

In this example, your startup cost is $5000. Rewards cost $20 to make in small batches, but about $15 to make once you are making a run of 1000 pieces.

50 supporters = $ 6000	Each Supporter: $ 120	
100 supporters = $ 7000	Each Supporter: $ 70	
150 supporters = $ 8000	Each Supporter: $ 53	
200 supporters = $ 9000	Each Supporter: $ 45	
500 supporters = $ 13,000	Each Supporter: $ 26	
1000 supporters = $ 20,000	Each Supporter: $ 20	

Looking at the chart, you will see that at 50 supporters, your PER PERSON costs are about $120 a person, while at 100 supporters, your PER PERSON costs are about $70 each. Once you hit 1000 supporters, that number is only $20.

In this example, you can clearly see that the more people who support the project, the lower the individual costs can be. This chart does not show any profit or extra money, because, at this point in the planning, we are only considering raw costs based on your budget.

Sample chart: Contingency and Fees

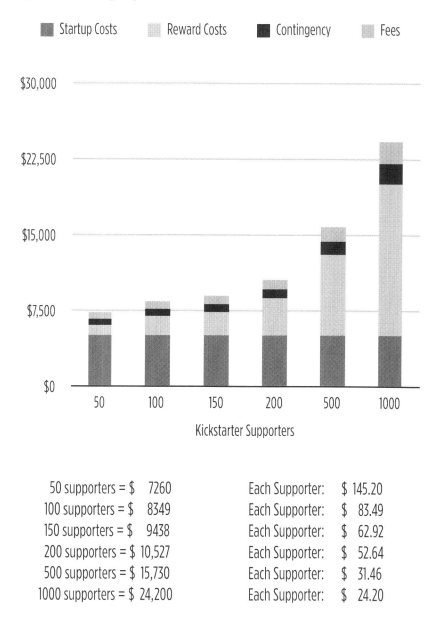

■ Startup Costs ░ Reward Costs ■ Contingency ░ Fees

50 supporters = $ 7260	Each Supporter: $ 145.20
100 supporters = $ 8349	Each Supporter: $ 83.49
150 supporters = $ 9438	Each Supporter: $ 62.92
200 supporters = $ 10,527	Each Supporter: $ 52.64
500 supporters = $ 15,730	Each Supporter: $ 31.46
1000 supporters = $ 24,200	Each Supporter: $ 24.20

With adjustments to add contingency (a little extra in case of problems) and site fees (around 10% of the total raised), the numbers are a little higher. But allowing for the plan to include some safety in your budget and to account for the fees in the cost of the overall budget, you can select the best level in which to set your goals.

Let's clarify our terminology.

VALUE: how much the supporter expects to pay for an item.
PRICE: how much the supporter will pay for a given item.
COST: what you will pay to have that time made.

Using the chart information to explain the pricing

At 100 supporters, it will COST about $20 to make each item. To reach your goal, each of those 100 people will need to pay a PRICE of at least $83.49.

If you are making something that customers value at $100, then you are doing really well. In this case:

VALUE	$100.00	How much the item should cost
PRICE	$83.49	Supporters pay less than they expected
COST	$20.00	You pay for the making of the item.

This is a great model, because in this case, your main reward has a higher VALUE than the PRICE. So you are on the road to convincing people to buy your item through Kickstarter, so that they get a discount.

When you meet and exceed your goal

People	Raised	Cost	Profit
100	$8,349.00	$8,349.00	$0.00
200	$16,698.00	$12,584.00	$4,114.00
500	$41,745.00	$15,730.00	$26,015.00
1000	$83,490.00	$24,200.00	$59,290.00

You only have one reward

When you begin the process of setting the price for your Kickstarter support levels, think about it as though you only have one reward and a lot of added items. In most cases, that will be true. If you make an iPhone case, that is your reward. If you make an album, that is your reward. A DVD is the reward for a film. Tickets are the reward for a performance.

Everything else is an add-on.

Using value and cost to set a price for your reward

Your reward will have a definite COST. To produce a DVD, it costs a certain amount of money. There are variables, like burning on your computer versus having the DVD replicated by a service provider. The COST, in your estimation, is the amount you pay to make and ship one DVD. Include shipping in the COST. So, if a blank DVD, case, insert, envelope and postage adds up to $5, then that is your cost.

The VALUE of your DVD is also something that should be determined. If it is a feature length movie, then a DVD might have a value of $20, including shipping. If it is a short film, then the value might only be $15 with shipping. The value is the judgment, determined by what people would likely pay at in a retail situation.

When you set your PRICE, you don't want it to exceed the VALUE, but it absolutely must not be lower than the COST.

If you are making a product

In the general market, the PRICE would be 6 to 8 times the COST of making the item. If your product has a COST of $20, then the PRICE could be up to $160. Judging where to set the PRICE is based on VALUE. If you believe that the value is $300, that is great. If the VALUE is only $35, then you have a very slim margin for profit and will need to sell a lot of them to meet your goal.

If you plan to sell the reward in the general market after the Kickstarter

In a wholesale environment, you would be selling the items at half of the retail price. So if you plan to make more than just the rewards for Kickstarter, you will need to know that. If the COST is $20 and the PRICE is only $35, then you would lose money on the wholesale items. Your PRICE would need to be higher or you would have to make the cost lower. Remember that you already accounted for shipping in the previous model, so perhaps the COST can be lower if you are selling in bulk. Also, your COST might be lower merely because you are producing a larger quantity.

How to make the meet the goal price

If you are making a short film, no one is going to pay $83.49 for a DVD or a download. So you need to consider how you can add to the reward to bring up the average VALUE on the rewards.

You could sell the DVDs at $15, with a COST of $5 each. For each one, you would make about $9 each, after 10% in fees. If your film cost $5000 to make, you would need to sell almost 650 DVDs to meet the Kickstarter goal.

The reason that there are levels of support on crowdfunding sites is so that people can choose to participate at the financial level that they can afford or at the financial level in which they perceive that the VALUE is greater than the PRICE.

In planning, you should recognize that some people may like the idea of your film, but only have $1 to give. Make sure that there is a reward level for them. A nice email thank you would be enough reward.

Create several low PRICE support levels, where supporters get something of VALUE to them, but with no COST to you. For example, a digital download has no cost, but has VALUE. A shout-out on twitter or facebook has no COST, but to some people, it is worth supporting you.

How the hell am I going to do all of this math?

Don't Worry

If you aren't a great math person or find this part a little overwhelming, then you are in luck. I created an online system to do the math for you. You can use this tool as you progress through the next few sections, to save you from all of the calculations.

What you need to know to use the online system:

1. Startup Cost
   This is setup of the project, making the film, recording the album

2. Cost to make ONE reward
   This is the cost to make one iPhone case, one DVD, one CD, etc.

3. Minimum to Make
   Do you have to make at least 100 items? 1000 items?

4. The Value of the reward
   What would people expect the retail price of this reward to be?

5. The Discount on Retail Price
   How much will you discount from retail (if at all) to get people to support?

Once you have those few things answered, then go to this website to have the math done for you.

www.secretsofcrowdfunding.com/math

The website form will tell you:

1. Your Kickstarter Goal
    This is the minimum goal amount that you would set to break even

2. The Number of Supporters
    How many supporters you would need if you only sold the reward as it is.

NOTE

If you want to give the math a shot, jump to the last page for the formulas.

Creating and Pricing Reward Levels

In the grand scheme of your project, planning your rewards might be the most important factor in your Kickstarter success. Of course, knowing that you will be able to complete the project is important, but being able to achieve your minimum goal is going to be a byproduct of creating attractive rewards at a variety of levels.

The most important factor in reward creation is INCLUSION. If you are making a film, then you want to appeal to the film lover in Iowa, in Mississippi, in Vienna, in Tokyo. You want to give them something that they can't achieve at home, because they don't have access to it. For a musician, giving demo tracks and live video performances of songs allows your supporter to hear the process of the song being finalized. It makes them an insider. And everyone wants to be an insider in a creative project.

Personal Rewards

A reward doesn't always have to be physical. It can be something that offers a personal touch. These more personalized items can be vary from a video message of thanks, to a Skype call, or a thank you in your album's liner notes. Handwritten notes are very nice and mean a lot to some people. Others want a little more glory and may be interested in giving a lot of money to have their name appear in the credits of your film.

Some of these personal rewards offer status and others offer a personal connection. But every one of them offer something more than just a copy or a product. They let the supporter feel connected to the project. And that connection is a great way to include people in your process and make them into grassroots cheerleaders for your success. A person who has their name in the credits of a film with tell friends and share on social networks. And, should they share during the fundraising process, they can help you to reach more people.

An Insider's View

Beyond giving them a credit or a phone call, you can also give them access to a look behind-the-scenes. Using a free blog, like Wordpress.com, you can easily create a website that offers updates and images showing the process of your project. Perhaps it may seem more applicable to creative works like films or albums, but there are plenty of supporters who want to see how you went about making your bluetooth phone adapter gadget as well.

Allowing your supporters to see your work-in-progress gives them an experience as well as a final product. It pulls back the curtain on the creative and business processes that they may not have known about before. And it allows them access to see something that they don't have in their day-to-day lives. That access is worth money.

Options and Decisions

Part of inclusion may be in offering your supporters a say in your decisions. However minor those decisions may be, it makes the experience even richer to have some kind of vote or opinion. Perhaps it is the final color of your iPhone adapter. Or it is the cover art for the CD, selected from three or four options that you share with the group. Maybe it is the movie poster or trailer.

Allowing for interaction with meaningful contributions takes the inclusion model to a far greater depth. It brings your supporters into the fold even further and strengthens their feelings about your campaign. They will go even further to share their positive experience with their personal contacts. And though much of that may occur after the initial campaign, it will be useful for a future customer base for your project when it reaches beyond the Kickstarters who helped you to get it made.

A great benefit of kickstarting your campaign is that you can capture support on a variety of interest levels and on a variety of financial levels. Each level of support can offer a different experience or reward, but can also cater to people of different financial capacities.

If your prices are too high, then you would keep out the people who might give you a few bucks because they like the idea. Someone with a $100 gadget might offer a $5 level for a thank you note or a logo sticker. It promotes involvement in the project for people who may not have $100 to risk at the moment.

Consider contribution as a risk

There is no guarantee through Kickstarter or any of the other sites that the project will be completed and that the rewards will be delivered. Remember that this isn't a direct purchase. So people might be hesitant to throw money your way. But in building a smart campaign and accounting for the reluctance of the potential supporter, you can often get smaller contributors who don't receive a full-priced item just because they want to be part of the process.

Identify the standard set of rewards and extras

If you are creating a 3-D Printer, then the printer itself is one of the rewards. Adding supplies, software, demo files, and bonus materials are the way to build up the rewards for higher levels.

For a musician, you can offer a CD or digital download. You might offer posters and t-shirts, additional songs that didn't make it to the album, remixes, videos, a book of lyrics, or a limited edition version on vinyl.

Films can offer DVD, BluRay or digital download. Again, the levels might offer materials much like the musician, with t-shirts and posters. You might offer director's cuts, commentary versions, or soundtracks.

For the board game creator, expansion sets are a wise way to build levels beyond the standard game.

In theatre or dance, a backstage pass, better seats, or a dinner package would make sense.

For fashion, limited edition versions in different colors or patterns become options when you are selling clothing. Besides the dress, offer a set of accessories. Beyond the shoes, offer different colored shoe string sets or different patterns on the soles. If you make sunglasses, offer a hard case and lens cleaner.

Decide on the standby bonus items

For any project, a t-shirt, poster, pack of stickers, or tote bag are logical and expected add-ons. Many of these things can be ordered in bulk and add value far beyond their individual costs. A t-shirt could be valued at $20, but only costs $5 to make. That is a smart addition to your project, as it increases the contribution level without the same increase in the costs. You are able to make profit here.

Look for companies like Jakprints.com that offer a variety of items that you can make to fulfill the orders. They print apparel, bags, stickers, posters, and more. You can even print underwear, should that appeal to you.

Offer something creative or limited

The more unique the offering, the more value it has. In many cases, you can find something that has value to a contributor that his a minor cost to you.

In a film, props or costumes can become great items to give away. A visit to the set would cost you nothing other than a couple extra mouths at the craft service table. Tickets to the premiere would be a nominal cost, but a great reward for a Kickstarter contributor. Walk-on roles are a great item, especially since it will help you with filling those crowd scenes without having to find extras.

For an album, tickets to the release party or a visit to the studio are great offers. A private concert, either in person or online could be great. A dedication of a song at an upcoming performance has value, but costs you nothing. Handwriting lyrics might sound silly, but a true fan would enjoy having something that you made specifically for them.

A phone call or Skype call with you, a cast member or a musician in your band might be something that get people excited. Knowing that they are interested in your project, they might have questions about your process. Or they might just want to get to talk to someone who they wouldn't have had access to before.

Perhaps a budding fashion designer is looking for advice. Face-to-face instruction (or via Skype) is a great way to include your supporters and to give them something entirely unique. A musician can teach you a couple chords on the guitar. Or they could learn a cover song to play for you.

One of a Kind Rewards

Making a one-of-a-kind reward is incredibly awesome. Knowing that you are the only one in the world with a dress, an iPhone adapter, a BluRay, or a painting. Much of Kickstarter is using your creativity produce something. If you can make one (or a few) that a limited number of supporters can have, that item is worth additional support.

Online Resources

There are some interesting sites online, like Ponoko.com which make laser-cut items in wood, metal and plastics. Using their online system, you could create something special for a supporter that no one else would have.

3D printing sites, like Shapeways.com, help you to create non-traditional items. Not only would this kind of site help in creating a prototype of a physical item, but could also help you to create one-off, exclusive items. Making a limited edition casing for your product using 3D printing might give you some additional items to share with your backers.

Customized or personalized items work exceptionally well. If you can include a name or picture on your final packaging or your website, people will enjoy being noticed. And that connects well to the elements of inclusion in your rewards.

Integrate the elements of inclusion

Remember that INCLUSION is the key to getting people to contribute their money now, rather than waiting to buy the product after it is completed. Beyond a discounted price, it is one of the few reasons to get involved.

In building your rewards, find ways to include people from the most basic level of support. Access to your password-protected Wordpress blog, which documents your progress is a really great start and a value to people. Behind the scenes photos and access, directors commentaries, demos, storyboards, and mockups are all part of the process and are all interesting to your supporters.

Start there and build the levels of communication. Update all of your supporters through Kickstarter, but give them more than just the occasional update. Take 20 minutes to write a thoughtful update and upload some images. It changes everything.

Think about other ways to include your supporters. Some will be limited to higher levels of support, like those Skype calls or one-on-one sessions. But some might be easier to accomplish for more people, like a video update you shoot on your phone.

15. The value of free

There are plenty of rewards that are physical items, like a bluetooth adapter or a t-shirt. But there are also many rewards which have no cost to the creators. For example, digital downloads are essentially free. Bandwidth is negligible, serving that information can be as simple as posting it on a yousendit.com or wetransfer.com system and sharing a link. Or even simpler, post it into a free wordpress blog system and share the link with your supporters.

For musicians and filmmakers, it makes it a really obvious choice to make your lower-level support rewards a digital download. That goes for authors, who can share a PDF or ePub version of their book. Fashion designers might share a pattern, so that the do-it-yourself, crafty types can make something at home. Video games might have bonus levels, different avatars for the players, or even soundtrack downloads. Some of those songs are really catchy.

Extending your product line with additional digital (free) items

For those of you who are making a 3D printer, where the base cost for the item is $2000, then free downloads are the bonus material. Pre-designed 3D printing files, so that customers can print right from the start, make a lot of sense. You can also offer 3D printed items, which demonstrates the value of your printer while also giving people who can't buck up $2000 the opportunity to have something printed for them. The marketing value of sharing 3D items you have printed is worth quite a bit.

Beyond the digital product

Adding a "Thank You" in a film's credits doesn't cost anything, but it has value. The same goes for being listed in a CD's liner notes. Some companies are even printing the names of their supporters on the product packaging. That is a super creative idea, and costs nothing more than what you were planning to spend.

Early Release

Getting something early is often enough of a benefit to encourage a supporter to get on board. Being first is something that we crave. Knowing that you will be one of the first to hear a CD or see a movie, that is a benefit that has no COST but has VALUE.

The Limited Edition Rule

Offering a limited edition version of a reward is a great incentive. Numbered, signed pieces often are perceived as more valuable than the general run. But there is also a danger in offering limited edition items. Once you have sold out of the limited edition, supporters need to still find reason to support the campaign and choose a non-limited reward. If not, then they might think that they could just wait and buy it after the product is made, when there is less risk.

When you offer a limited edition item, make sure to create that limited edition as a double incentive. Once it is sold out, then the second incentive is still in place for other supporters.

If you are making a camera lens to attach to smartphone cameras, perhaps one lens comes in Arctic White instead of the standard Piano Black. The limited nature of the product is only a color, so once it sells out, the value of the standard version is still in place.

Get it First

Several campaigns offer "first in line" editions, which would be the same product but shipped to those supporters as early as possible. So, if there were 1000 products to send and the first 100 products arrive at the facility, they will go to the Limited Edition supporters, while others would have to wait until the later batches arrive.

This is a combination of the early release and limited edition models. There is no change in COST, but there is a definite increase in VALUE. Even a few more dollars to offer people a "first in line" release can really help to reach your goal faster.

Building and Launching Your Campaign

As you are developing your Kickstarter project, but considering where you will be posting information about the campaign.

Social networks

It is only logical to start with your friends and family. They are going to be the first people who will help you to get started, but don't rely on them for the entire project. Ask them to support you, but also ask that they SHARE your campaign with their social networks. If all of your friends on Facebook share the campaign, you are reaching hundreds, if not thousands, more people.

Tell people you are going to launch a campaign before it goes live. Prepare them. And let them know what you are asking of them. You need for them to get the word out for you. It is more valuable than their financial support. They need to be the first people to begin spreading the word. And ask them to share the launch of the campaign and at least one more time during the campaign. The repetition will reinforce that it is something they believe in. And it many people will miss one of the posts and will hopefully click on the second one.

With Twitter, and other networks you have the same opportunity. Ask for the retweet. Ask people to share with their followers.

Your website

If you have a website, use it. Make sure that there is at least a page of information about the project. Use the Kickstarter widget to show the progress. Make sure it is easy for people to click to the campaign directly.

Blogs

Don't just rely on your own blog, since you probably are reaching the same people as your social networks. Do a bit of research and find blogs which focus on products or projects like yours. Look for news outlets who might want to cover the concept. People like to be the first to find a great new idea or project. Send them the info as soon as the site is live and ask them to post about it.

Print Media

If you have an inside track in the print world, then use it. If you have enough advance notice, you could have the article or blurb appear during the campaign. But realize that print doesn't have the speed of the internet and there are no easy buttons to press to get people to your Kickstarter campaign. It is a bigger stretch, so don't expect a huge response.

A Kickstarter page is broken into sections, like most of the crowdsourcing websites. There is a video, a content / text area, a goal area, and a rewards area.

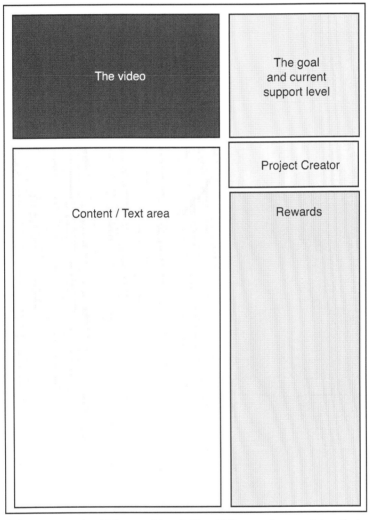

Each of these areas should be considered. The GOAL area is something that you can ignore when you are building, as it is automatically created. But the Project Creator area, which is also created based on your account, may be a concern.

Project Creator Area

If you have never supported a Kickstarter campaign before, that will be information that people will see. It may not matter in the long run, but showing that you are part of the community, supporting other projects, will give you an advantage.

The rest of the areas of the page are created in the process of building the page.

When you are creating your page, the video is going to be the most important introduction to your campaign. It is the chance for you to reach out and show what you are making, to engage the Kickstarter community, and to begin a relationship with your supporters.

Planning the video

Your video should be long enough to cover what you need to say, but not too long. The average user doesn't have 10 minutes to watch your video. They probably will give you 2 or 3 minutes before they make their decision. In your planning, try to cover the most important features in the beginning, so that supporters will get the overall concept and can make a decision even if they don't have the time or the attention span to watch the entire video.

If you are a filmmaker, your video is even more important. If you are expecting people to give you money to make a film, then you certainly have to prove to them that you can make a video for the site.

Equipment is everywhere

Your video can be shot on your phone. You don't need anything more professional than the camera on an iPhone or even on most webcams on the computer. Don't expect that you will need a crew of people and the latest filmmakers' gear. You just need something to hold the camera still on the shot, like a tripod.

Sound is key

You can squint your eyes to try to see better when a video isn't clear, but when sound isn't clear, you can't "squint" your ears. Make sure that the place you are shooting is quiet enough that you can be heard clearly. Do some tests. If there is too much echo, put some blankets on the floor and the walls. If there is too much noise from outside, then close the windows or find another space. Turn off air conditioners and things that will cause an annoying hum.

Show and Tell

When you are doing your video, you should concentrate on showing as much as you can, rather than telling. People expect that you will be explaining your idea, but the more you can show them the better. Most people are visual learners. While they can imagine something when you explain it, the task is greatly simplified by showing them images.

For rewards that are products, like clothing, gadgets, or artwork, then your video should be showing the demo items. Even non-working models are better than nothing. The sample clothing on a mannequin or model, the iPhone case rendered on a computer and shown in 3D, the sketch for the artwork or the first pieces in the series... all of these things will be a benefit to you if you show the supporters, rather than explaining what you are planning.

Musicians can show music videos or performances. They don't have to play all of the new songs, but showing that you have played before and what your style is, that should be enough. If you can demo some of the new songs, 20 - 30 seconds, then you are ahead of the game.

Filmmakers don't need to show a movie that they haven't shot. But they can show pictures of the cast, storyboards, designs, costume ideas, etc. They can bring a cast member in to talk about the film. They can talk to writers, directors, cinematographers, or any key crew member.

For live performances, it is important to let people know where and when the performance will be. Show an empty stage, but explain what kind of transformation will happen for the show. Remind people that the performance is live, so it would be geographically difficult for a supporter in San Francisco to come to a show in Denver, unless they make the trip.

Tone

The feeling that people get from your video is your chance at a first impression. How you craft those feelings is through the tone of the video. When you are creating a product, you should be positive and excited, but not overboard. You don't need cheerleaders to get people engaged, you need to present your product with conversational tones, with a bit of fun. A smile goes a long way.

Humor

Humor sells. If you are creating a heavy drama, then the jokes won't fly. But a lightness to the video will engage the viewers far more than a cold, dry overview of the project.

The Ask

You MUST ask for money. The people who are watching the video know that you are creating the project and are pre-selling the idea. If you don't ask for money, then you are dropping the ball in the middle of your play. You need to ask, politely and appreciatively, but directly. Invite people to join your project, to be involved, to support you.

Video Guidelines

1. Show as much as you can. Tell the rest.
2. Inform the supporters about the project.
3. Keep the video short, so that you keep their attention.
4. Match tone to project. Keep it light.
5. Be appreciative. Be thankful for support.
6. Ask for the support, to be part of your campaign.

---

19. The Content Area

Your content area shouldn't be a transcript of your video. Instead, it should cover the same information in bite-sized sections. Realize that at times, people may not be able to watch the video. Whether they are on a mobile device with slow internet or at work without speakers or headphones, your content still needs to do its job.

Where to begin

Start with a project overview. Tell the supporters what the project is and what the final product would be. If you are making a short film, your overview is that you are making a short film and will be delivering a finished HD film. For a musician, it is recording an album and delivering 12 songs.

The story of the project

Following up on the overview, tell a little about where the project originated. The idea for your gadget came when you realized that you needed something to hold your phone when you were taking photos. Or the film is a fictionalized version of how I found the right dog to adopt.

The features

In the case of a product, this is where you tell about why the gadget is so great. For clothing or shoes, this is the stand-out parts, which set these designs apart from other clothing. For a film, this is the actors or other talent that would encourage people to support.

The details

After showing off the best parts of the project, you can go into detail about the project. This could be a bit about the making process and how that works.

The rewards

This would be a little bit of information about the rewards. If you can show the rewards, do it. Pictures sell more than just a description. You don't need to re-list all of the reward details, since they will be on the column to the right.

About the money

Remember to ask for the money. At the end of the page, tell people what the money would be used for, what the extra will do for the project, and how you would feel if the project didn't reach the funding goal.

When you build the content area, you should consider the different kinds of people who are reading the information. It is not just considering the people, but the way their minds work. Sounds odd, but people consume and evaluate information differently. And your page should be ready to cater to each of those types of people.

Spontaneous

There are spontaneous people, who will just support a project that looks good without looking very closely. They are the type that buy things at the checkout area in the grocery store. They are the type who accept a snap judgment of a project. They are covered just by having a page and a title.

Humanist

There are the humanists, who look to what other people are doing. They are the type who look for the reviews of movies or check out the before and after pictures on a website to make their decisions. They will commit to your project if you have a lot of people supporting you already. And they will commit if someone cool says you have a good idea. So look for a person who might validate your project, whether it is a talent or a blog or a publication.

Overview

Most people are overview types, who read the headlines and then decide whether or not they need to read any further. These are the people who don't jump at buying something, but are easily convinced about the benefits or features. If they are satisfied with the headline, they don't need more information. To cater to those people, each paragraph of the content area needs to have a headline and that headline should be bold. It should be a good representation of the content of the paragraph.

The more bite-sized the information, the better.

Detail

People who need every detail will already have plenty of information on your Kickstarter page. They will read every word on the page, watch the entire video and review all of your rewards. These are the type of people who read ingredients and research using consumer reports before buying a tv or a car. If they read all of your information and are satisfied, then they will be more likely to support the project.

It never hurts to add more images. But the content can't be just images. Certainly, you should treat the images as reinforcement of the text that is on the page.

Photos or videos in the text

Using photos in the text is relatively easy. You want to choose small images that highlight something you are explaining on the page. Beyond the video, the additional images can help guide people through the information.

Inserting a picture is pretty easy. There is a button on the Kickstarter page that allows you to easily insert an image or video.

Additional videos

When you think of using additional videos, remember to keep them short. Each one can give a bit more depth to a feature of your project. If your main video is an overview of the features, demonstrate the feature completely in a separate video. If someone wants to know more, they can watch. But there is no obligation to watch all the videos to get an idea of what the project is. The video should compliment the other material, but shouldn't be required. Most people won't spend the time to read and watch everything.

Mockups and storyboards make great additional material. Since you haven't made the project yet, these images can give more confidence in the project.

You only have one reward. All of the rest are add-ons.

This is true for many projects. Some, like fashion design, may have different rewards. But the concept remains that you are creating a project and the product of that work becomes the reward. A CD of your music is a reward and so is a digital download. They are different formats of one reward.

An example of Add-Ons

In order to build the campaign to best raise your support, just offering the reward would mean that you only have one option. And as appealing as that may be, add-ons offer additional income from a supporter. Think of it this way, your CD and a poster and a t-shirt become one level of support. The VALUE of that level is $15 for the CD, $5 for the poster and $20 for the t-shirt. The COST of that level is $5 for the CD, $1 for the poster and $5 for the t-shirt. All together, the VALIE is $40 and the COST is $11. Your supporter will be giving $29 directly to the making of the project. If they only bought the CD, you would only be getting $10.

Profit Margin

The difference between the VALUE and the COST is the profit margin. In you were planning to make an album, you expected a profit margin of $10. So the digital download was $10 and the CD was $15, to cover the cost and shipping. When you build your levels of support, you ALWAYS create them so that the profit margin is higher than $10. That way, you decrease the number of supporters needed when people decide to support at the higher levels.

Naming the levels of support

As you build the levels, you should give them a name. The classic- Platinum, Gold, Silver and Bronze - differentiate the value of the level by associating with precious metals. In your campaign, you can differentiate using any family of names that would build such associations.

Why name them? Two reasons. First, a name provides for a simple reference. You don't want to have to say "the level with the video and the dvd and the shirt and the poster and the stickers" when you could say "Movie Lover." Second, by implying that another level has additional value, through the gradually more impressive name, then you are inspiring people to reach a little higher and support the level above the one they originally choose. It is subtle psychology, but it makes use of our inherent need to get the best version we can afford.

Let's be honest. No one likes spelling mistakes. Check over your page for grammar and spelling. If you aren't a good editor, have someone else look over it.

Review your rewards and make sure that the reward level is correct, as is the description of what is in the package. If the second reward level includes all of the items from the first reward level, make sure that it is clear.

Simple enough. Launch. Press Go. Make it happen.

Start Promoting

On Day 1, you can go crazy in promotions. Send your emails and post to the social networks. Ask everyone to repost your link.

On Day 2, go crazy again, since many people might have missed it on day 1.

On Day 3... STOP. Don't go overboard.

A promotional calendar

Keep the updates spread out. If you reach your goal quickly, you can post and tweet a thank you. That would be awesome. Otherwise, don't be pushy.

When people support your campaign, post a "thank you" on their wall or tweet a thank you to them. Your campaign is thanking them as well, through the automated email system.

During the campaign, post updates on the Kickstarter page. Don't post them privately. Make sure that people who visit the page can see when you are updating your supporters so you demonstrate that you are communicating with the team you are assembling.

You can post once a week to your networks until the final week. In the last few days, you can post once a day.

If you reach your goal

Only post to tell people that there is still time to be included. Don't be greedy. Don't look greedy. If your product is something people really want, they will continue to support it long after the goal is met.

The End of the Campaign

25. If You Reach Your Goal

Once you reach your goal, Kickstarter will charge all of the supporters. You will need to be in contact with supporters whose credit cards don't clear. Simple messages will help to make sure that everything works.

In about 2 weeks, the money will be deposited into your account. It will be the total of the campaign, minus the fees.

In the meantime, you can be working on your project, confident in the knowledge that the cash is coming. Start production.

It is now your job to make and deliver as you promised. Congratulations. You succeeded and people believed in your project enough to give you money before you even began.

You are responsible for following through. Don't let your supporters down.

Review your campaign and see where it failed. This is a great opportunity for you to see why it didn't work.

Most campaigns fail because of reach.

Kickstarter isn't part of the world's daily routine. It is still new technology and a relatively new concept. You are educating many people as you are asking them to support your campaign. Over time, that will change.

Is it just a bad idea?

Another reason, bluntly put, is that people don't like the project. Does that mean that it is a bad idea? No. Does that mean that the people you reached don't want it? Yes.

This is a serious part of evaluation of the project. There are going to be ideas that aren't great. And maybe yours is one of them. Talk to people. See what they think of the idea. Ask them to point out the flaws.

Bad timing

If you launch and then the stock market crashes, then it is bad timing. But there are other factors in timing besides the market. Perhaps there are other, competing projects that got people more interested than yours. Or maybe it is too close to the holidays, so people had their money tied up in other things.

Maybe you came across negatively

Did your campaign make you look greedy? Did you seem too cocky in the project? How people react to your campaign directly affects their support. Again, ask people to review the work and see if you came across kindly.

Unclear goals or rewards

Maybe they just didn't get it. Was your campaign clear in what you were making, when it would be delivered, how it would be of benefit to the supporters? Was it a gadget for the iPhone 3GS, but no one has that anymore? Was it a film that was too experimental? Did you decide to become a musician, but didn't share any samples of the style?

No unique factors

Perhaps people didn't find the difference in your project compared to another project. Or they don't see the difference between your project and another project in the general market.

Make sure that throughout the process, you are communicating with your supporters. It will help keep them engaged and happy. Let them know when rewards are shipping and always keep an eye on the messages on Kickstarter to see if they communicate with you.

Part of what makes your project exciting is the promise of inclusion. Deliver on that promise, because supporters will become the grassroots cheerleaders of your finished project. Once the album gets to the supporters, they will be the ones posting about it on their networks, telling their friends how great it is. And they will be the ones who are proud of being part of the making of the process.

I haven't stopped telling my friends about the watchband for my iPod, the bluetooth adapter that saves my Bose Sound Dock from becoming obsolete, or the documentary about the beautiful life and tragic loss of Tom Bridegroom. I am always hoping that the creative projects I find (and can afford to support) will succeed and that I will be able to benefit from the project as well.

Though it isn't quite ownership, crowdfunding offers participation in the creative process. And the more included the supporters, the more personally invested they are in the result.

The next time you are ready to launch a creative venture, you will have a collection of people who were treated well, given what they were promised, invited to spend time in your world. And the next time, they will have even more confidence pressing the button, putting their financial support behind you, telling their communities and networks that you followed through on the last one... and you'll do it again.

Kickstarter and each of the other crowdfunding sites are the best kind of use of technology. They offer a gateway for people to share their ideas and their creativity. And they help artists, who generally aren't very business minded, succeed at both their art and at making a living.

Throughout history, great artists have often had patrons, who believe in their abilities and support them financially. They may have been wealthy families or individuals, government programs, churches, or charitable organizations. Now, it is the world at large, the crowd, who come together to support the creative.

Entrepreneurs and artists will find that they have their place in the crowdfunding community. And those of us, like me, who love to discover the projects... well... we have our place too. And that place is made all the better when a campaign becomes a joint venture between the dreamers and the believers.

Worksheets and Examples

When you are planning your rewards, take a look at each level and add up the COST and compare that to the PRICE. The COST should always be less. The difference, or profit margin, should be larger and larger, as your rewards get more and more expensive.

When you evaluate each add-on item, look at the overall profit margin to see if it is worth making.

Example: Remember : PRICE - COST = PROFIT MARGIN

REWARD	COST	PRICE	PROFIT MARGIN	EVALUATION
t-shirt	$5	$20	$15	good reward
sticker	$.25	$1	$ .75	not so great
vinyl record	$45	$40	-$5	bad reward

In this set, you see that the t-shirt has merit, because you profit at $15 each time you sell one. But the sticker, it only makes you $.75. You would need to sell 20 stickers to make what you make from ONE t-shirt.

And the vinyl record loses money. It may be a great reward, but not at that price. You would need to find a less expensive source for the reward or raise the price on the reward to make it work.

NEVER offer a reward that doesn't make money. Losses will eat away at your project money. You don't want to have to sacrifice your project's integrity because you couldn't plan your reward levels correctly.

The following pages are worksheets so that you can write out and evaluate your add-on items.

REWARD	COST	PRICE	PROFIT MARGIN	EVALUATION
_____	____	____	____	_____
_____	____	____	____	_____
_____	____	____	____	_____
_____	____	____	____	_____
_____	____	____	____	_____
_____	____	____	____	_____
_____	____	____	____	_____
_____	____	____	____	_____
_____	____	____	____	_____
_____	____	____	____	_____
_____	____	____	____	_____
_____	____	____	____	_____
_____	____	____	____	_____
_____	____	____	____	_____

REWARDS WORKSHEET

PRICE - COST = PROFIT

REWARD	COST	PRICE	PROFIT MARGIN	EVALUATION
_____	_____	_____	_____	_____
_____	_____	_____	_____	_____
_____	_____	_____	_____	_____
_____	_____	_____	_____	_____
_____	_____	_____	_____	_____
_____	_____	_____	_____	_____
_____	_____	_____	_____	_____
_____	_____	_____	_____	_____
_____	_____	_____	_____	_____
_____	_____	_____	_____	_____
_____	_____	_____	_____	_____
_____	_____	_____	_____	_____
_____	_____	_____	_____	_____
_____	_____	_____	_____	_____

30. Examples

Example project #1: SHORT FILM

STARTUP BUDGET

From pre-production through post-production, to get a final copy of my film, I will need to spend $7500.

THE REWARD and THE COST

The reward for a film is a copy of the film. I am going to use the DVD as my basic reward. It will cost me $2.85 to burn the DVD, print the insert and put it in a case. It will cost me $2.15 to mail. So, my COST is $5.

HOW MANY DO I NEED TO PRODUCE?

I can do just 1 DVD, so that is my minimum.

THE VALUE

I think people would spend $10 to get my short film shipped to them.

THE DISCOUNT PRICE

I am not going to offer a discount. Seems a bit weird on this, since I am not selling it at retail prices later.

THE MATH

Using the online formula from www.secretsofcrowdfunding.com/math I find that I need to set my goal at $20,950.

WHY?

When I make the film, I need to recover $7500. And for each DVD, I am only making $5 in profit. And remember, I have to pay fees on everything I bring in, so I am really only making $4 on each DVD I sell. That means I have to sell 2095 DVDs to break even.

Let's look at the math again.

2095 people spend $10 each to get me $20,950.

I pay	$2284	in fees (around 7.9%+$.30 on each transaction)
I pay	$7500	to make the film
I pay	$10,475	to make and ship DVDs ($5 each)
	————	
TOTAL	$20,259	

Why is there a difference of $691?
In the calculations, there is a contingency amount added to the budget, in case things don't go smoothly and the project requires a bit extra. Here, it is close to 10% of the cost of the film, but less than 5% of the overall project amount.

If the filmmaker sticks to the budget, that money becomes profit. If things go a bit over, then they are covered.

Example project #2: Zoom Lens for Mobile Phone Camera

STARTUP BUDGET
In order to make the casing, source the lenses, get the assembly team together, design the packaging... that is going to cost $12,775.

THE REWARD and the COST
The reward is the Zoom Lens. It is going to cost $8.85 for each lens.

HOW MANY DO I NEED TO PRODUCE?
The production company requires that I make at least 1500 pieces in the first run. After that, I can do shorter runs of the product if I need to.

THE VALUE
Another company is selling a lens like this but it only works on older phones. Theirs is $75. Mine is better. I would place the retail price of my lens at $70 so that I can compete.

THE DISCOUNT PRICE
I really want people to buy this early, so I am going to offer $14 off that price, a 20% discount for people who get it on Kickstarter.

THE MATH
Using the online formula from www.secretsofcrowdfunding.com/math I find that I need to set my goal at $30,362. And I only need 543 people to buy the lens at that price to break even.

WHY?
There is a minimum number to produce in this plan. 1500 lenses need to be made. With a $56 PRICE and only $8.85 COST, that means $47.15 in profit for each lens sold. When I reach my goal, I will have 957 EXTRA retail-ready lenses already paid for.

Let's look at the math again.

543 people spend $56 each to get me $30,408.

I pay	$2538	in fees (around 7.9%+$.30 on each transaction)
I pay	$12,775	to start the project
I pay	$13,275	to make 1500 lenses
TOTAL	$28,588	

Why is there a difference of $1900?
In the calculations, there is a contingency amount added to the budget, in case things don't go smoothly and the project requires a bit extra. Here, it is almost 15% of the cost of the startup, a little more than 6% of the overall project amount.

So if everything goes perfectly, there is $1900 in profit and 957 retail-ready lenses at the end of the project, if the Kickstarter goal is met.

If you have no minimum to produce...

((STARTUP COST) + (**100 SUPPORTERS*** COST))/ **100 SUPPORTERS** = COST PER PERSON

When COST PER PERSON = DISCOUNTED RETAIL PRICE you have it right.

Try more or fewer supporters until you the numbers are equal.

Once they are equal, use that number of supporters

((STARTUP COST) + (SUPPORTERS * COST)) * 1.05 * 1.10 = Kickstarter GOAL

(including contingency and fees)

If you have a minimum to produce...

((STARTUP COST) + (MINIMUM* COST))/ **100 SUPPORTERS** = COST PER PERSON

When COST PER PERSON = DISCOUNTED RETAIL PRICE you have it right.

Try more or fewer supporters until you the numbers are equal.

Once they are equal, use that number of supporters

IF THE NUMBER OF SUPPORTERS IS LESS THAN THE MINIMUM...

((STARTUP COST) + (MINIMUM * COST)) * 1.05 * 1.10 = Kickstarter GOAL

(including contingency and fees)

IF THE NUMBER OF SUPPORTERS IS MORE THAN THE MINIMUM...

((STARTUP COST) + (SUPPORTERS * COST)) * 1.05 * 1.10 = Kickstarter GOAL

(including contingency and fees)

Made in the USA
Lexington, KY
22 August 2013